Little Rays of Sunshine

Ashley Merkes

BookLeaf
Publishing

Presentation by *BookLeaf Publishing*

Web: www.bookleafpub.com

E-mail: info@bookleafpub.com

ISBN: 9789357744843

First edition 2023

*To every lost soul out there trying to find
their way in what seems like a world of
darkness. Keep the flame in your sights. It
will not burn out, it will only shine brighter.*

ACKNOWLEDGEMENT

I would like to start by thanking God. Without God, none of this is possible. Thanks for the nudges and nods along the way.

I want to thank my mom and pops for being as excited about this book as I am, their love and patience with me, and for always letting me know I'm never too old to come home. Evan and Andrea for being my safe haven, always hyping my ideas and nudging me past my fears. Aidan and Aspen for helping me see the magic of the world through their eyes. My grandparents, I love and miss you dearly and hope I am making you all proud up there. My aunts, uncles and cousins who have loved and helped me through some of my darkest days - whether they knew it or not.

Abbie, Karli, Lauren, Sara, Steph (and their beautiful families), Kaitlin, and all my Leroy girls (you know who you are) - thank you for being my chosen family and loving me for who I am.

Krysta and family, you always make me feel loved and like one of your own. Every party, vacation, and bonfire has been a true gift. I wish everyone had a family like yours in their lives.

Kayla, thank you for weathering storms together, believing in me, being my travel buddy, and loving all the kooky parts of me - especially the ones I'm too afraid to share with the world. You get me and I'm forever blessed to have you in my life.

Kristen, my soul sister. You are a huge part of why I chose to write this book. Our adventures and travel assignments (especially NYC) lit up my world and gave me newfound courage. I'm eternally grateful.

Samantha Hanson, who taught me that I must first unpack from the journey, then separate the laundry and put away the souvenirs before letting go.

Brittany, thank you for breathing belief into me and always seeing that I could do whatever I set my mind to. To the #inspirebeauty team: my thanks for helping to shape me into a woman who is brave enough to face her fears and slay her dragons.

Kippi, thank you for inspiring me and giving me the confidence to take this leap.

Shout-out to The Open Door Coffeehouse. I have spent many afternoons drinking iced matcha lattes and writing here. The welcoming warmth from your shop, and the people within, is felt. Your love for the community always inspires me.

My work fam. You make me laugh every day. Thanks for being the best cheer squad out there!

Thank you to BookLeaf Publishing for the incredible opportunity to publish this book full of poems - they have been in my heart for years. Fate brought me to you and I am so very grateful.

Finally, a huge thank you to everyone who has encouraged me, taught me, and believed in me. There are so many. As I sit typing this, I am thinking of you all - teachers, classmates, co-workers, strangers who extended kindness - each of you has made an impact in my life.

PREFACE

Sometimes what we feel is expressed through the words we cannot say out loud.

Souls

Where do all the broken souls go?

They roam and walk among us

Searching the shadows

Hiding in plain sight

In crowded rooms

And whispered undertones

Lonely crowded sidewalks

Subway stations bustling with noise

They are you and I

For aren't we all a little broken?

The Monster Beneath My Bed

I grit my teeth,
I try to forget.

The pictures in my mind keep playing -
There is no "off" switch.

Like a movie stuck on repeat,
Images flicker by.

The monster that haunts me refuses to leave,
Laughing at my terror, paralyzing me.

Mom and Dad can't save me from this,
A dark hidden secret I've tried to forget.

Smiling away the pain for years,
I mastered playing pretend.

A false sense of safety eclipsed the shadows,
Checking beneath the bed no longer mattered.

Monsters lurk and linger,
They never fully leave.

I open my eyes from this nightmare,
But it's my reality.

In Bloom

the little petal dreamed of being a flower
bright blossoms swaying in the breeze

bumble bee friends frolicking in the sun
fragrant perfume floating in the air

large raindrops fell on the petal
dewy droplets threatened to trample

the storm passed
in its wake something magical

rainbow stripes lit up the sky
the world illuminated with color

the little petal began to bloom
one by one brilliant, bright blossoms grew

strong and sturdy
bending with the wind

she took what was dealt to her
and came out stronger in the end

The Angel

an angel came to visit
as I lay in bed
she floated near
beautiful and loving
so very ethereal
through the darkness
she cast a glow
giving endless comfort
to take with me where I go

Sunset

The sky is on fire

A bold change is in the air

Darkness falls away

Scrapbook

Fresh mountain air
Tall, sturdy pines
Warm croissants with strawberry jam
Shooting stars streak across the sky

Waterfalls rushing
Boats drifting by
Cool water in the lake
Family by my side

Prairie dogs waving
Nearby horses whinny
Sun warming my skin
A lifetime of memories carried within

Blue

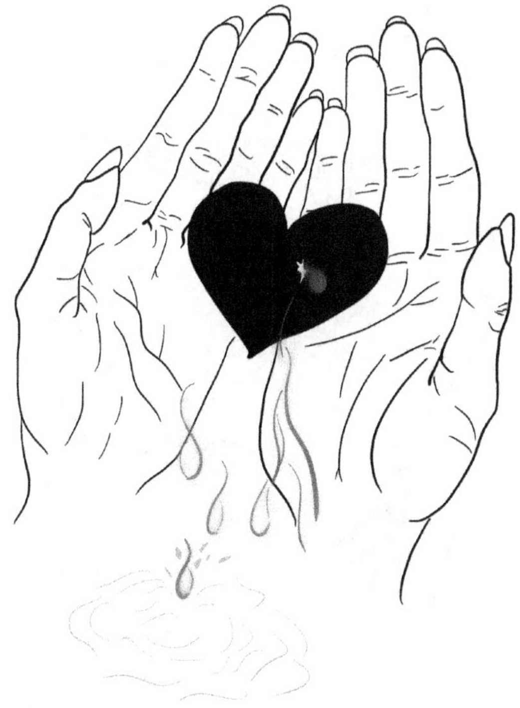

Just the memories live

Once electric blue

Stayed away, but never far

Holding my heart, protecting us all

The Guardian

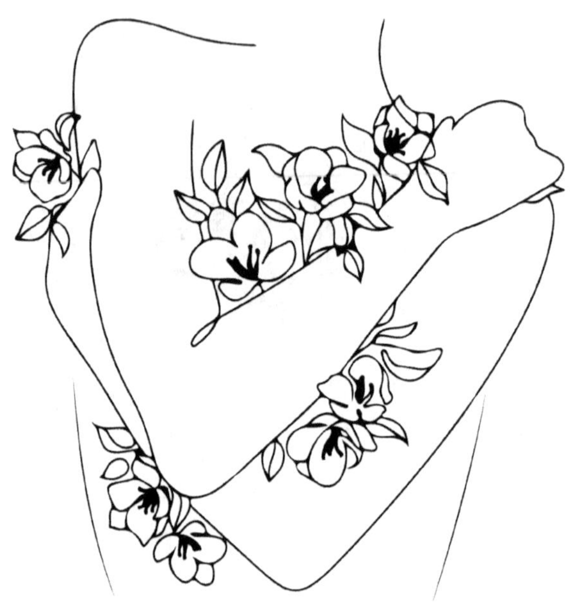

I find you

in the unexpected monotony
and every miraculous moment

I hear you

as breezes whisper through my window
and in the lyrical songs I sing

I feel you

take hold of my hand
guiding me to safety

I miss you

days and weeks
and months turn to years

I know you

forever a part of me
walking beside me

Rock Shows & Halos

Safety in spaces still exists

A couch in a basement

Cruising in a car

Rock music raining down

Slaying inner demons

An oversized black t-shirt

Two broken beings

Someone who understands

When the time has come to leave

Thank you...for saving me

October

stars lighting up the sky
open field beneath our feet
clean, crisp autumn air
hookah smoke rising
not a cloud in sight
time is standing still

Oceans

Waves crash brokenly

The siren song calls to me

Oh, won't you come in?

Interlude

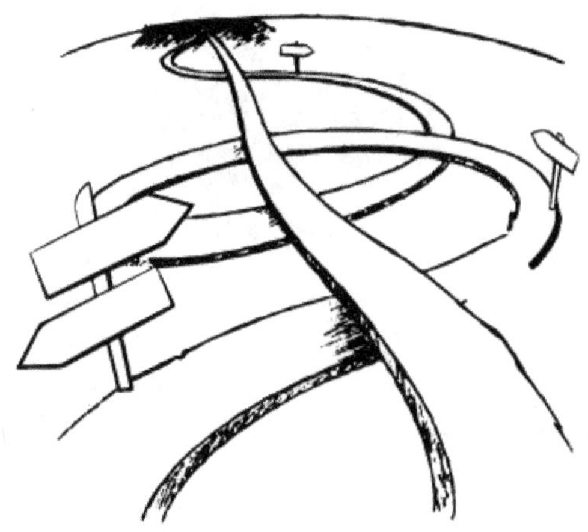

New cities, sites and sounds
Sometimes fearing
I'd never leave the ground

Pack it up and drive
Coast to coast highways
Never felt so alive

Survival mode for too long
Breaking free
Fixing what was wrong

Heart bursting wide
Breathing in life
Beautifully tragic, wild ride

Delaware

Friday,
the thirteenth day of November

Precious soul,
you changed our worlds forever

My heart,
how could it have known?

Love,
unconditional, pure, renowned

New magic,
flooding the earth

Gazing at life,
through eyes lit with mirth

Dragonflies

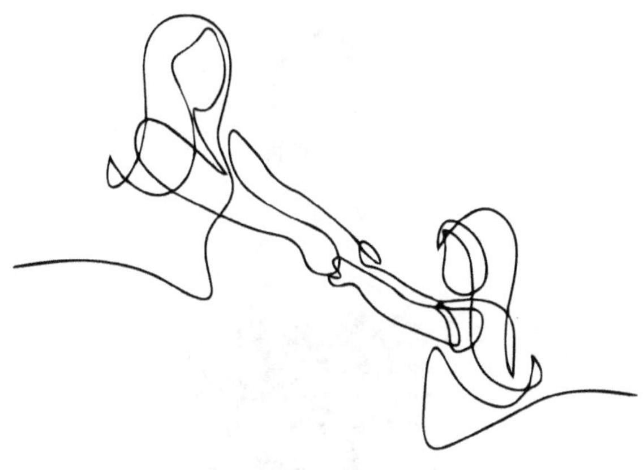

Alive and vibrant

Uniquely beautiful

Nearby messenger

Transformation complete

Little Leaf

the aspen leaf shimmers
glorious and bright
her beauty brings a glimmer
dawn breaks through the night

unicorns and fairies dance
magically with glee
life is one great game of chance
wistful, beloved, free

Cali Roll

Heart beating fast
A caged butterfly's wings

Trapped in my ribs
Will it break free?

Grasp at each fleeting moment
Sand runs through my hands

Never meant to be
No longer part of the universe's plan

Currents

emptiness in the noise

loneliness in a crowd

building like a tidal wave

this feeling never leaves

the current is pulling

small chance of resurfacing

needed here

tugging me far away

leaving forever

ghostly vanishing

a chained heart

afraid of splitting open

when all that's loved is lost

how does one fight the current?

The Great Masquerade

Give enough of a smile to gain their trust,
force a laugh to choke down the really dark
stuff.

Outwardly calm and happy,
chaos coursing within.

Keep it up - gotta hide,
when someone asks, just deny.

Lying in bed,
drifting to space.

No will to get up,
tempted to give up.

Numbness sets in,
locked in a cage.

Convinced they won't care,
if all that's left is a name.

Masquerade and disguise,
my Dr. Jekyll and Mr. Hyde.

The Wish

Blowing out the candles
Whispers cross my soul
Dreams of happily ever after
Upon the golden knoll

Smoke rises up
Candles all blown out
Life is of your choosing
Wishes pouring from the spout

Night

I stare up toward the heavens

Cloudless, starry night

How can all of this exist?

Life's marvels and its plights

A deep inhale reassures me

I've never been alone

All the darkness in the world

Beauty knows no bounds

Exhaling on a whisper

Tears fill up my eyes

I feel you standing with me

As I gaze up at the skies

Sunshine & Ash

this is 32 years
breaths…moments…fears
emerging from the dark
go on, live on a lark
demons finally put to rest
heaviness removed from my chest
opened my eyes to newfound restoration
the promise of life's unbound exploration
so much left to be uncovered
a whole world yet to be discovered
should I leave here on the morrow
shed not a tear of sadness or sorrow
rainbows, love and harmony exist
painting rays of sunshine through the abyss

www.ingramcontent.com/pod-product-compliance
Lightning Source LLC
La Vergne TN
LVHW010835200726
843508LV00012B/2607